TEACH US TO PRAY

SHARDELL MARTIN

Shardell Martin

Copyright © 2021 by Shardell Martin

All rights reserved. No part of this book may be reproduced in any manner whatsoever without written permission except in the case of brief quotations embodied in critical articles and reviews.

First Printing, 2021

Teach Us to Pray/ Shardell Martin
ISBN
978-1-7378760-9-0
ISBN
978-1-7378760-8-3

Shardell Martin
Facebook Shardell Martin
Instagram @shardellmartin
shardellmartin@hotmail.com
unless otherwise indicated, scripture is taken from the King James Version.

TEACH US TO PRAY

CONTENTS

Foreword — vii
Dedication — ix
Acknowledgements — xi

1. Chapter 1: Reason why to pray — 1
2. Chapter 2: How prayer can help you — 3
3. Chapter 3: Praying through difficulties — 5
4. Chapter 4: Praying after Victory — 8
5. Chapter 5: Seeing God as a person — 10
6. Chapter 6: Praying from and for purpose — 12
7. Your job is never done — 14
8. Chapter 8: Anybody can pray — 16
9. Chapter 9: Do I know how to pray? — 18
10. Chapter 10: How to pray — 20
11. Chapter 11: Am I an intercessor? — 22
12. Chapter 12: Do it again!!! — 25

About Author — 27
Reference — 29

FOREWORD

Prayer has been and is a lifeline to me. The things I had to face and overcome in life I would not have been able to do without being able to turn to God in prayer. It helps keep me going. Prayer has been and is a place of refuge, a safe place where I can get away and be in peace. It's one of the tools the Lord has used to change, heal, develop, correct me, and most importantly keep me connected to Him. Prayer is not just something you do but it can be a place you live in, Psalm 91. Prayer has been and is a place I go to solve problems, release problems, get worked on, get strength, counsel, instruction, direction, help, comfort, insight, understanding, encouragement and more. It's a place where I know I'm welcomed to and belong, fit in, always open, and can get to from anywhere. It's a place I know I'm loved, wanted, appreciated, and needed. If you are reading this and if you have not experienced these things I have spoken of, well you also can have this, these are some of the experiences that await you in God. In this book I will give you simple tips, insight, instructions, and more that can help you start, enhance, or deepen your prayer life/ experience with God and bring you closer to God. Also, to help you understand the mind and heart of God. No more Praying from desperation, out of religion, and or tradition but, it's time to pray from a place of intimate relationship with God the Heavenly Father.

DEDICATION

This book is dedicated to the readers. Those who may have felt like it's hard to hear from God or build a strong relationship with Him. To those who know you love God but struggle in finding or living for Him. Last, but not least, to those who want to learn how to pray, or improve and grow in their conversation with God.

Enjoy!

ACKNOWLEDGEMENTS

My Grandmother Emily Martin: You were the first to introduce me to and teach me how to Pray. Our Father prayer and lay me down to sleep. Thank you for teaching me and the other grandchildren prayer.

Late Bishop Raymond Lee and Pastor Geneva Lee: I can remember attending intercessory prayer on Monday evenings and watching you all walk the floor, lay on you all face, do warfare and more. Thank you for allowing God to use y'all to lay a foundation and love for prayer.

Prophetess Kimberly Martin: Watching you go before God to not just pray but do it with fire, fervency and prophetically changed and encouraged me to pray. Thank you for imparting that and helping me be bold in prayer.

Apostle Phillip Green: God has used you to teach me so many things. Thank you for teaching me how to press and seek God through fasting and prayer.

Apostle Davidson: For pushing me to do this book and your **Wife Apostle Davidson** for covering me in love and prayer.

Bishop Nash: Who would let me come to your church freely to pray and meet God. Thank you for believing in me.

Prayer partners and pushers in different seasons: Prophetess Shakila Kendall, Prophetess Mary McNair, Prophetess Elizabeth Whitfield, Prophetess Ronda Terrell thank you all so much, you all helped me through some hard and dark times. Much love.

Apostle Lakeisha Savage: Whether it was watching you from far via social media or attending one of your glory encounters services. The Lord has used you greatly in multiple ways. Thank you for the sacrifices, hardship and pain you went through to get the oil and glory God has placed on your life, to help birth out and push farther, people like me who do not know you personally but love and appreciate you greatly!

B Copes: You were used by God, to wake me up out of religion, pain and the hurt that I was running from and come alive to my authentic self. Thank you. I'm forever grateful for you.

Finally, Hardship and Process: Thank you for pressing and pushing me to seek and draw closer to God. You helped me grow and pray so much and not because I always wanted to, but I had to. So many complain about you, but I thank you because I would not be who God destined me to be without you.

CHAPTER 1

Chapter 1: Reason why to pray

Why, why, why? Why do one pray? When does one pray? Where do I Pray? How do I pray? All good questions that will be answered in this book. Is prayer for certain people? Can one pray, if they don't believe in God?

In this chapter I will give you the reasons why to Pray. First, we all should pray because everybody needs God. If you are a creation, then you need God. We were created to need God. It's built in us to be in relationship with God. Prayer is one of the main ways of communicating with God. If or when one doesn't pray as a lifestyle it causes distance in the relationship with God. Prayer is what helps build and maintain a relationship with God, get to know God and oneself. It's how we can get help, direction, instructions, clarity, peace, comfort, and so much more. One won't be rightly aligned in life without maintaining a prayer life with God through Jesus Christ. Prayer helps us to examine ourselves to see where we miss God standards in our life and where we are measuring up. Prayer and the word of God helps build you up, encourage, strengthen and keep you focused. Prayer is a place where one can find God. Where one can talk to Him as well as God communicates back. Only thing prayer costs is time. Are you willing to make the time / invest your time to get what you need? It's not enough to know you need God, but you must want Him. The way you know you really want God is by seeking Him out. Prayer is a place to not only seek God but to find Him. By reading the word of God, fasting, praying, and being a true servant of the Lord. These are ways of seeking out God.

Ending Conclusion: why I pray? There are many reasons why I pray, and I will share a few. I pray because not only do I need and want God, but I can't imagine my life without Him. God is the reason why I live. To me, a life without God is not a life, it's just existing.

CHAPTER 2

Chapter 2: How prayer can help you

A big part of what and who I am is because of what God can accomplish in prayer. It's too much to count of what can be accomplished in prayer. There is nothing too small or big to pray about. Prayer is one of the ways we can allow God access to help us. Jesus said anything we ask in His name, He will do **John 14:14**. Prayer is the vehicle to help get things done. Prayer can (if you allow God to have His way) fix you mentally, emotionally, physically, occupationally, spiritually, socially, get your mind right, balance you out to see things the right way, strengthen you, build up your confidence and take you where you belong and more. I ask again how can prayer help you? It helps bring you into the right relationship with God, yourself and others. It's impossible to develop an intimate relationship with God without prayer. Prayer is one of the healthy and right ways to examine yourself through the Spirit, heart, and mind of God. It's one of the tools God uses to develop us into His image, likeness and our authentic selves. Prayer helps you become the real you and fulfill the purpose and destiny God has for you. Prayer helps you to release your burdens, worries, frustration, toxicities, false perceptions, and mindset. Prayer helps you to grow up and mature. It's one of the main ways to fight your battles, hardships, weakness and more and win. It's the place of victory, to overcome, get strategy, encouragement, direction, instructions and more.

Ending conclusion: That's right, prayer is not just something you do but it becomes a place where your soul and Spirit get connected back to the source that created it. It's a place that is beyond human reasoning and comprehension. A place of peace, joy, rest, and most importantly a place where you meet God.

CHAPTER 3

Chapter 3: Praying through difficulties

Difficulty: the quality or state of a thing that is hard to accomplish, deal with or understand. When faced with difficulties how do you handle it? When dealing with difficulties, pray it through and do not stop. Of course, this is easier said than done, but it is doable. Difficulties are a reminder that we need God. If we are honest, with most people when things appear to be well in our lives, we forget God. We forget God in a lot of ways. Whether it is in our thoughts, our response to situations and people, the way we do things, our decision making, lifestyles, time, and more. The bible tells us to acknowledge God in all our ways and He will direct our paths **Proverb 3: 6.**

Most times we do not acknowledge God when we're going through things because we do not know Him enough and or we do not want to do things God way. It's when we humble ourselves and ask God for His help and receive this help (by doing things His way), then He can guide us through the difficulties of life. Most times when we ask God to help us, we want Him to make the situation end and sometimes He does that and then it's times that He won't. The things He won't take away are the difficulties we need to make us better, the things to prepare us for God's purpose for our lives, the things He teaches us to show us ourselves, the things that show us He's God in spite of us, the things that build us up and more! When we continually pray to God, He will show us how to overcome and direct us. He will be a guide through what appears to be difficult to us. As we learn and trust in God we come to see, what was once hard for us to deal with becomes easy because God graces and strengthens us to handle and overcome it. Yes, there will be a lot of mixed emotions, clouded judgement, wrongful thinking, times you want to give up, respond the wrong way, moments of depression and more but know that God will bring you through. I can say that because God brought me through many difficult situations from bad relationships, homelessness, health issues, death of loved ones, failed goals/ dreams, and more. God continues to bring me through difficulties. When dealing with difficulties you have to decide if you are going to take on the mind of the victim (woe is me mentality/mindset/ feeling bad for yourself) or victorious mindset (what lesson I need to learn and what changes I need to make so I can overcome this). The biggest part/thing of handling difficulties is your perception. How do you see it? *(Perception: a way of regarding understanding or interpreting something, a mental impression.)* Jesus said, "for as he thinketh in his heart, so is he" **Proverbs 23:7.** If you take on the mindset that I can't do this, it's too much, or the victim, that is what you will get, defeat! If you say I can do all things through Christ who strengthens me **Philippians 4:13.** Greater is He that is in you, than he that is in the world **1 John 4:4**. If God be for us? **Roman 8:31.** Then you will have victory. The bible says the power of life and death is in the tongue **Proverbs 18:21.** Speak life and get victory. Know that you can handle any difficulty if you turn to God and do things His way and not yours.

End conclusion: Some of the things I learned from dealing with difficulties are it is wise to be mindful of who/ what you turn to for counsel, comfort and help. Who or what you turn to can be a temporary fix that makes things worse or can prolong what you're dealing with. Not everyone understands what you're dealing with or are designed to help you in your time of difficulty. The more you rely on God the more help you get from Him, whether it be strength, encouragement, realignment, restoration, clarity, understanding, wisdom, directions, solution, grace and much more. To continually turn and talk to God is to pray it through. Every time you turn to Him something is changing even if it's you that is changing. The more you change for the better the more you become equipped to handle and overcome your difficulties.

CHAPTER 4

Chapter 4: Praying after Victory

Praying from a place of victory should not produce pride but humbleness and gratefulness. As one reflects on what God has done and is doing it produces an attitude of gratitude. Fruit of real victory has been won, when one takes on the Spirit of God's fruit. Not pride, acting or thinking you did it or thinking you're better than, or bragging on yourself **Proverb 27:2** Let another man praise thee, and not thine own mouth; a stranger and not thine own lips. That's a sign of false victory, vainglory, and your battle has not been won **Philippians 2:3** Let nothing be done through strife or vainglory; but lowliness of mind let each esteem other better than themselves. **Victory is designed to change us.** God's glory or things being done to the glory of God always reveals God, and points people back to God, and not man or self. Victory is the celebration of what God has done and how He uses you through the process to accomplish it. Victory is to build us up and encourage us to keep trusting, relying on and doing things God way. It's a reminder of what God did and can do.

Ending conclusion: Victory humbles the pure in heart because they know who they are apart from God because there is no Victory without Him. Victory is not just the time to celebrate the goodness of the Lord and what He has done but God I'm thankful for what you did for and through me, now what's next? So don't become stalled or stuck in yesterday's victories but now is the time to ask, "God what will you have or like to do through me next?"

CHAPTER 5

Chapter 5: Seeing God as a person

As I think on this topic I smile because this is how my relationship with God grew tremendously. What does it mean to see God as a person? One example; when it comes to a romantic relationship with man and woman- when a woman is into a man and she knows she is about to meet up, go out, or see the man she is feeling or love, she makes sure she presents herself well. Hair done, face clean, fresh breath, hygiene good, smelling good, outfit/ clothing right and so on. Same thing for a man when he is feeling a woman, he makes sure he puts in the effort to impress and lets it be known he wants her. Fresh haircut, hygiene right, car clean, breath fresh, gear/clothes right, sneaker fresh and so on. With that being said we need to see God the same way. Meaning we treat Him like a person we see as being valuable to us. Which entails, when it's time to pray we make sure we don't go to prayer any type of way. If we're looking to develop a better relationship or intimacy with God. I like to wash my face, brush my teeth, hygiene right, on time, not distracted but focus, with reverence, humbleness of heart and mind, knowing that He's God (nobody or thing is greater than Him). It's a privilege and one of the greatest honors that's been granted to mankind to be able to access Him through His son Jesus and the Holy Spirit.

Even when its prayer time making sure it's quality, priority time. Not in a rush to leave His presence or coming for a handout like God's a genie in a bottle, or sugar daddy. But Lord, how can I serve you today? Is there something I can do for you? How can I live a life that's pleasing to you Lord? Last example: when seeing God as a person, know that you can talk to Him about anything the way you would someone you trust and have your best interest at heart. Someone who is not going to betray your trust. You can talk to God knowing you don't have to be perfect and know scriptures, just tell Him what's on your mind and heart. Tell Him about your difficulties and the things you experience or go through and cannot tell anyone else. Whether you pray out

loud, quietly, standing up, sitting down, walking, working, however and wherever, just talk to Him and allow your relationship with Him to grow. Eventually you will go from talking to God for 2 mins to 20 minutes until it's hard to keep up with how much time you spend with God, because you just love talking to Him.

Ending conclusion: know that with seeing God as a person it will help you develop more awareness and consciousness of God. You'll start one way praying and as you continue in prayer you will find you're changing for the better as a person and in your relationship with God. You will find yourself talking to God anywhere, anytime, or at night and in the morning in your head until it develops to you not just having a set time you meet God but prepare yourself to meet God.

CHAPTER 6

Chapter 6: Praying from and for purpose

When you find yourself praying from and for purpose it's a place/mindset of knowing what God has called or chosen you to do in life and you communicate to God based on what is needed for that purpose or to fulfill that. That can look like God changing you, your ways, people you hang or be with, the way you think or do things, atmospheres, places you go, things you do and so on. What is purpose? ***Purpose: is the reason for which something is done or created or for which something exists; An intended or desired result.*** When praying from a place of sincerity and pure motive for purpose, it is a place of selflessness. Giving up your desires and will is what it takes to fulfill the will of God. God created every person for a purpose so when one looks or seeks out God for this, one is looking to take their rightful position with God on the earth. That's what praying for purpose is about looking to align your life, desires and will, in exchange for God's will, desires and plan that He has for you (which is much better than what we could want for ourselves). When praying from the place of purpose there are rights/benefits and requirements that come with it. God helps you to fulfill that purpose in many ways, whether it's providing resources, sending people to assist you, giving you strength, direction, instruction, wisdom to get it done His way, encouragement, grace, and much more. Living out what God created you to do is one of the places where true happiness, and fulfillment comes from. Praying according to or from purpose is one of the keys to praying effectively. One can pray all day long or all the time, but the question is, "Are you praying effectively?" Are you praying for the right things?" The goal when praying from or for purpose is to be effective. One will always be effective when praying God's will, with the right motive and intent, God's timing and in faith. If one doesn't believe or have faith, then one must check why they are praying.

Ending conclusion: Understanding God and how He thinks don't just help you in prayer but in life. Everything God does, did or allows serves a greater purpose that's beyond you. You weren't just created for God's purpose but something that was greater and beyond you. The closer you get to God, the closer you get to not only knowing and understanding your purpose but yourself. And God said, Let us make man in our image, after our likeness **Genesis 1:26.** You were created to be like God. What's greater than that?

CHAPTER 7

Your job is never done

As an intercessor your job is never done. Being an intercessor is a lifestyle so even when you see prayers being answered you don't stop praying, you keep going. Although God does allow us to rest, there is always something to pray for. People are desperately in need of God, especially the one who thinks they don't need God. They need our prayers the most. The bible says, satin is making great havoc because his time is short **Revelations 12:12**. Because of this, the altar of incense must stay lit **Luke 1:11**. This is not a job for one person, but for all those who will say yes to the call to be intercessors. And I sought for a man among them, that should make up the hedge, and stand in the gap before me for the land, that I should not destroy it: but I found none **Ezekiel 22:30**. The number one requirement of an intercessor is to be available for when you get a call/job from God's Spirit to pray concerning a matter. Intercessors are so important because we have a say in what will or will not happen by saying yes to God when God says it's time to pray. As an intercessor it's a must that we pray God will and not our own. God counts on us to be a part of making His will happen on the earth **Matthew 6:10**. Intercession is a behind the scenes' job that gets rewarded openly. Jesus said pray in secret and my Father will reward you openly **Matthew 6:6**. This is a job that has room for unlimited growth and requires maximum obedience. The more you obey God the more you grow and elevate in access on many levels. There is always a need for intercessors of all ages. No one is too young or old to pray. It doesn't matter your race, background etc. God has a need for us all. So, will you say yes to the lifestyle of an intercessor?

End conclusion: There are different stages and levels of intercession whether you're a beginner or intermediate, it's always room for growth. So don't compare the way you pray to someone else instead come to learn the way God wants you to pray. Most importantly say yes to God, get started, and keep going. Watch how and what God does through you!

CHAPTER 8

Chapter 8: Anybody can pray

That's right, anybody can pray. It doesn't matter your age, color, height, size, background, past, present or future etc. God loves us all! For God so loved the world, that He gave His only begotten Son, that whosoever believe in Him should not perish, but have eternal life **John 3:16**. God created mankind with the intent to have a relationship with Him. God invites all people to come and talk and build a relationship with Him through His son Jesus Christ and prayer. So much so He named His house/temple, "A house of prayer for all people," **Isaiah 56:7**. We are God's desire that He longs to be one with. We were made to be one with God and to be disconnected or unreconciled with God is to be disconnected from yourself. *Reconciled: to restore to friendship or harmony, to what is broken.* Through us coming to God we get fixed, we get put together the right way (His way), how God originally created us to be in His image and His likeness **Genesis 1:26**. I love going to God because I feel safe with Him, loved, accepted, I can rely on God, I can talk to Him about any and everything, I get honest, and loving feedback from someone who I know has my best interest at heart and won't steer me wrong. I love spending time with God. It is one of my favorite things to do. He has always been there for and with me, through good and bad things, hard times, dark times, and trying times. He just wasn't there but He was my strength when I needed it, counselor, healer, (physically, mentally, emotionally, occupational, socially, and Spiritually) director, gave me wisdom, a friend, protector, provider, father, mother, comforter, and more. I don't just need God, I want Him.

Ending conclusion: I invite and welcome you to come and get to know this God I brag about. Even if you already know Him, in what way have you not learned Him yet that you can get to know Him? Or how can you strengthen or make your relationship with Him? Come He's inviting you to come pray.

Heavenly Father I pray a special prayer for those who will accept you, I invite them to come to you, that you grace them to seek you, and give them a new thirst and hunger to know you better I ask that you allow them to feel your presence that is drawing them right now, touch their hearts and give them what to say in Jesus name I pray Amen.

CHAPTER 9

Chapter 9: Do I know how to pray?

The word of God lets us know in **Romans 8:26**, we don't know what we should pray for as we ought but the Spirit itself maketh intercession for us. Some people know how to pray and some don't, but the question is, if one knows how to pray do you know what you should pray for? I remember a few years ago, after already praying for a good amount of years, I found myself like Jesus' disciples saying, "Lord teach us to pray," **Luke 11:1**. I found myself before God and not assuming because I'm anointed, a leader, and knew how to do things good according to man standards, (preach, pray, teach, prophecies etc.) that I didn't need my Heavenly Father to teach me how to do things His way. When it comes to knowing how to pray, one may know how to pray but is it how God wants you to pray? It's not how many scriptures a person says, or length of time, if they are loud, or soft, etc. but it's about allowing God to pray through you by His Spirit. You pray at your best when it's God Spirit leading you into and through prayer. Don't model how you pray behind how someone else prays but simply ask God to teach you how to pray and give you what to say. God uses us all differently, so be ok with it and embrace it so that you may grow and develop in how you pray.

Ending conclusion: When you pray, ask God to make you more sensitive to His Spirit and presence. When He does make sure you yield to the leading of His Spirit. Because this is God answering your prayer to teach you how to pray. Remember who can better teach you how to talk to them then the person you're talking to. It's the same thing with God, no one is better at teaching you how to pray than God himself, so learn how to be and grow by relying on God.

CHAPTER 10

Chapter 10: How to pray

When one is praying to God, one can start by first acknowledging who they are addressing for example: God, Lord, heavenly Father, Father, God etc. Then one can either go into why or what they are praying for, or one can give praise to God for example: Lord I thank you, Heavenly Father you are great and greatly to be praised, God I thank you for waking me up today, etc. Lastly when one prays even in the beginning, middle or end of prayer one says In Jesus name I ask, pray, come to you etc. The reason for this is 1. Jesus is the way one must go through to get to God. 2. Jesus said anything we ask the Father in His name it will be given **John 14: 13-14.** Lastly ending prayer with Amen: it means so let it be or I agree. This is one of the most basic but effective ways to pray and get started. Remember it's not about focusing on the length of time or how well you speak but it's about your sincerity and giving God quality time by giving Him all of your attention during your time of prayer. This method will get results.

Ending conclusion: Here are some example prayers for the instructions: Heavenly Father in the name of Jesus I thank you for your goodness to me and how much you love me I ask that you teach me how to pray the way you want me to and teach me how to have a better relationship with you in Jesus name I pray Amen.

Lord, I come to you because I want to get to know you, the real you so show me the way and how to be committed to you first. Thank you for hearing me and in Jesus name I ask Amen.

God thank you for having my back, I know you are real and exist but I'm not sure of my purpose and I ask you to reveal it to me and that I may please you in Jesus name I pray Amen.

CHAPTER 11

Chapter 11: Am I an intercessor?

Intercessor: a person who intervenes on behalf of another, especially by prayer. Anyone can be an intercessor and there are some who are graced and anointed by God to be an intercessor. When one is called/graced/anointed by God to be an intercessor there are subjects that God gives them to focus on in prayer. Whether it's families, neighborhood's, health, leaders, nations, finances, evangelisms, violence, world events etc. There are so many different things to pray about, these are just a few examples. The life of an intercessor requires one to be selfless and on call. Selfless because one must sacrifice their time, fasting, sleep and more. You have to be on call because at any time God can require one to be inconvenienced to pray. Being an intercessor is very important and rewarding. This position requires one to be focused, trustworthy and reliable. An intercessor is granted access to God and privileged to insight. Intercessors are bold in prayer, faith driven, and know that God bears witness and will answer their prayers. Intercessors often fill the burdens of the Lord. Meaning the things of God's heart or things bothering Him. They are Sensitive to the realms of the Spirit and the presence of God. Abraham, a man of great faith and father of many nations, was an Intercessor. So the Lord said, "If I find in Sodom fifty righteous within the city, then I will spare all the place for their sakes. "Then Abraham answered and said, "Indeed now, I who am but dust and ashes have taken it upon myself to speak to the Lord: Suppose there were five less than the fifty righteous; would You destroy all of the city for lack of five?" So He said, "If I find there forty-five, I will not destroy it." And he spoke to Him yet again and said, "Suppose there should be forty found there?" So He said, "I will not do *it* for the sake of forty." Then he said, "Let not the Lord be angry, and I will speak: Suppose thirty should be found there?" So He said, "I will not do *it* if I find thirty there." And he said, "Indeed now, I have taken it upon myself to speak to the Lord: Suppose twenty should be found there?" So He said, "I will not destroy *it* for the sake of twenty." Then he said, "Let not the Lord be angry, and I will speak but once more: Suppose ten should be found there?" And He said, "I will not destroy *it* for the sake of ten." So the Lord went His way as soon as He had finished speaking with Abraham; and Abraham returned to his place **Genesis 18:26-32.** Abraham pleaded with God on the behalf of the righteous because he had the heart of God. As an intercessor it's important to know and pray to the heart and will of God in order to take on God's heart concerning people. Just as God doesn't take pleasure in people perishing neither shall we **2 Peter 3:9**, but is longsuffering to usward, not willing that any should perish, but that all should come to repentance. As an intercessor our prayer can cause people and nations to come to repentance. Intercession is about seeing God's will be done on the earth. Will you allow God to use you to bring His will to the earth? Here is an example of a man (**Nehemiah**) who allowed God to use him as an intercessor and more to bring God's will to the earth. That Hanani, one of my brethren, came with men from Judah; and I asked them concerning the Jews who had escaped, who had survived the captivity, and concerning

Jerusalem. And they said to me, "The survivors who are left from the captivity in the province are there in great distress and reproach. The wall of Jerusalem is also broken down, and its gates are burned with fire." So it was, when I heard these words, that I sat down and wept, and mourned for many days; I was fasting and praying before the

God of heaven. And I said: "I pray, Lord God of heaven, O great and awesome God,

You who keep Your covenant and mercy with those who love You and observe

Your commandments, please let Your ear be attentive and Your eyes open, that You may hear the prayer of Your servant which I pray before You now, day and night, for the children of Israel Your servants, and confess the sins of the children of Israel which we have sinned against You. Both my father's house and I have sinned. We have acted very corruptly against You, and have not kept the commandments, the statutes, nor the ordinances which You commanded Your servant Moses. Remember, I pray, the word that You commanded Your servant Moses, saying, 'If you are unfaithful, I will scatter you among the nations; but if you return to Me, and keep My commandments and do them, though some of you were cast out to the farthest part of the heavens, yet I will gather them from there, and bring them to the place which I have chosen as a dwelling for My name.' Now these are Your servants and Your people, whom You have redeemed by Your great power, and by Your strong hand. O Lord, I pray, please let Your ear be attentive to the prayer of Your servant, and to the prayer of Your servants who desire to fear Your name; and let Your servant prosper this day, I pray, and grant him mercy in the sight of this man" **Nehemiah 1: 2-11**. Not only did he carry the burden of the Lord, but he also fought for his people, he fasted, prayed, repented, cried out, and allowed God to give him wisdom, favor, instruction, and more to be the solution to bring God's will to the earth **Nehemiah 2:1-8**.

Ending conclusion: When we're willing and obedient to God and doing things His way there's no limit to how God can use us, so let God use you without limits.

Father I thank you and pray for all those who you will allow to read and touch this book that the limits will be removed from them, and the intercessor will awaken, and rise to new heights and depth In Jesus name I pray Amen.

CHAPTER 12

Chapter 12: Do it again!!!

Ready, set, Go- are you ready to do it again? Ok so you have seen or are seeing prayers being answered, but can you stay in that position? The position of allowing God to keep using you and growing you up to give you more challenging and advanced prayer assignments. Can you get results in the new place, from glory to glory **2 Corinthians 3:18**, requires you to grow as a person and intercessor? Will you keep going without interruption in the place of transition? Going from the place of seeing quick results/ prayers being answered to the place of wait and travail takes going the distance and endurance to see the results. Can you handle that? Yes, you can, you were built by God to advance and grow. You just have to keep believing in spite of you (your emotions, what you feel, think and see). This is the place you get focused all the more, limit and cut out distraction and allow God to become your strength. Because this transition is designed to make you more reliant upon God. This place will take you from caterpillar to butterfly, no matter your level. It's only God that will get you through this and the help He authorizes to help you. Get ready to become a new person. In this place you will not only do it again, but you will do new things, beyond you, that will have you saying, "only God can do that." This place is called, "no flesh can get the glory," **1 Corinthians 1:24**. It's a beautiful place because you come to know the authentic you that goes beyond your limitations and expectations, but the person God knew was there all along, but you needed God's process to become that. **Smiley face.**

Ending conclusion: God does everything lovely in His own time **Ecclesiastes 3:11** so don't rush but enjoy the process and stay close to God through it. Learn what God needs you to learn so you don't have to keep repeating the lessons, until you learn it. Don't be hard on yourself but do be accountable to God. He's watching anyway. Believe in yourself and God to the fullest. Remember to protect your relationship with God and what He gives you!!!

ABOUT AUTHOR

Shardell Martin is a God-fearing woman, and mother of two beautiful children. Who was introduced to God at age 22, and pregnant with 2nd child. Being in a place of hopelessness and no way out, the Lord introduces Himself to her through an answered prayer. Shortly after, she got saved and filled with the Holy Spirit and was on fire and dedicated to the Lord that day forward. Shardell Martin is a Godly purpose driven woman, who has a passion for the youth, overlooked, intercession, and God's will being done. She loves helping and building up people. Not only is she a voice for the heart and mind of God, she Pastor Daughters of Virtue ministries, leads different community outreaches, entrepreneur, author, tv broadcaster, active in her community and more. Shardell Martin is a firm believer of living a life that reflects and glorifies God. She knows her mission is to show and point people back to God, His will, righteous alignment, and good stewardship. She knows God has chosen, ordained, prepared, equipped, and bestowed His wisdom upon her to accomplish His will for her life. She accepted and looks forward to hearing, "Well done thou good and faithful servant: thou hast been faithful over a few things, I will make thee ruler over many things: enter thou into the joy of thy Lord." Matthew 25:23

REFERENCE

"**Difficulty**"- https://www.merriam-webster.com/dictionary/difficulty

"**Perception**"-https://www.google.com/search?rlz=1C1CHBF_enUS886US886&ei =cOBPYIiPMLqx5NoP8uSgwAM&q=perception+definition&oq=perception&gs_ lcp=Cgdnd3Mtd2l6EAEYATIKCAAQsQMQRhD5AT-IFCAAQsQMyBwgAELED EEMyCAgAELEDEIMBMggIABCxAxCDATIICC4QsQMQgwEyBQ-gAELEDM gUIABCxAzIICAAQsQMQgwEyBAgAEEM6BwgAE-LADEEM6BwgAEEcQsA M6DgguELEDEIMBEMcBEKMCOgIIADoLCC4QsQMQxwEQowI6CAguE-JEC
EJMCOgsILhDHARCjAhCRAjoHCC4QsQMQQ-zoFCC4QsQM6BAguEEM6Cgg
AELEDEIMBEEM6BAgAEANQ_BxYkDZgzFBoAnACeACAAdMBiAHnB5IB BTguMi4xmAEAoAEBqgEHZ3dzLXdperABAMgBCcABAQ&sclient=gws-wiz

"**Purpose**"-https://www.google.com/search?rlz=1C1CHBF_enUS886US886&ei=f OBPYIeQEtKg5NoP2PixyAM&q=purpose+definition&oq=purpose+definition&g s_lcp=Cgdnd3Mtd2l6EAEYADIKCAAQsQMQRhD5ATICCAAyBg-gAEAcQHjI
GCAAQBxAeMgIIADICCAAyBggAEAcQHjICCAAyBggAEAcQHjIG-CAAQBx
AeOgcIABCwAxBDOgQIABANOgkIABANEEYQ-QE6CwgAEAcQHhBGEPkB UJvuCli5lwtg-LoLaAFwAngAgAFoiAHTB5IBBDE1LjGYAQCgAQRGqAQdnd3 Mtd2l6yAEKwAEB&sclient=gws-wiz

"**Reconciled**"- https://www.merriam-webster.com/dictionary/reconcile

"**Intercessor**"-https://www.google.com/search?rlz=1C1CHBF_enUS886US886&ei =uOFPYIX6FfWu5NoPipuM2AM&q=intercessor+definition&oq=intercessor+defi nition&gs_lcp=Cgdnd3Mtd2l6EAEYADICCAAyBggAEAcQHjIG-CAAQBxAeMg
IIADIGCAAQBxAeMgYIABAHEB4yBggAEAcQHjIGCAAQBxAeMgYI-

ABAH   EB4yBggAEAcQHjoHCAAQsAMQQzoHCAAQsQMQQzoE-
CAAQQzoKCAAQ
sQMQRhD5AToECAAQDToJCAAQDRBGEPkBOgcIABCxAxAKUIUl-
WIM-Y   OhQaAFwAngAgAGrAYgB4waSAQQxMS4xmAEAoAE-
BqgEHZ3dzLXdpesgB
CsABAQ&sclient=gws-wiz

www.ingramcontent.com/pod-product-compliance
Lightning Source LLC
Chambersburg PA
CBHW072210100526
44589CB00015B/2460